Olivia Lauren's
A GUIDE TO THE
THINGS WE WEAR

Olivia Lauren & Melissa-Sue John

Illustrated by

Simonne-Anais Clarke & Zachary-Michael Clarke

Dedication

*To our multicultural friends living
around the world.*

*Allan Caseman, Izoduwa Uwague, and Melanie Aiken,
for their inspiration.*

*Sabrena Bishop, Lionel Emabat, Chanelle Harrigan, Dalton Richards,
Alkisha Pereira, and Sharlene Rajan for valuable feedback.*

Library of Congress Cataloging-in-Publication Data
Lauren, Olivia and Melissa-Sue John
Olivia Lauren's Things We Wear/ Olivia Lauren and Melissa-Sue John
Illustration by Simonne-Anais Clarke and Zachary-Michael Clarke
Summary: A multicultural and practical way to learn about the things we wear.
ISBN-13: 978-0-9979520-1-8
ISBN-10: 0997952016
Title I. Series. (Volume 5) Olivia Lauren
1. Clothes 2. Diversity 3. Culture
2017909713

Lauren Simone
PUBLISHING HOUSE
www.laurensimonepubs.com
@laurensimonepubs

Hello Friend! It's me, Olivia Lauren. I am at a fashion show. I get to model on the runway. My friends and I have a great idea. Let's explore the things we wear!

There are many names for the things we wear. They can be called attire, apparel, clothing, garment, gear, outfits, wear, or wardrobe.

The things we wear serve a purpose. We wear things for expression, protection, or tradition.

We wear things over our clothes to protect us from the cold, wind, rain, or snow.

Adam wears a **puffer coat.**

Indira wears a **parka coat.**

Taj wears a **faux fur coat.**

Xavier wears a **pea coat.**

When it rains, we wear waterproof things such as **rain coats, rain ponchos** , and **rain boots**

rain coat

poncho

rain boots

to prevent clothes from getting soaked. Kayla loves the rain. Taj notices that Harriet does not.

We wear fitted and stretchy clothes to exercise and play sports. Shawn, Xavier, and Rosa enjoy being active.

gym wear

sports gear

athletic gear

When it is hot, we wear loose and light things.

T-shirts, jumpers, and sneakers are my favorite things to wear in the summer. Harriet loves dresses and sandals. Rosa prefers tank tops, capris, and flip flops.

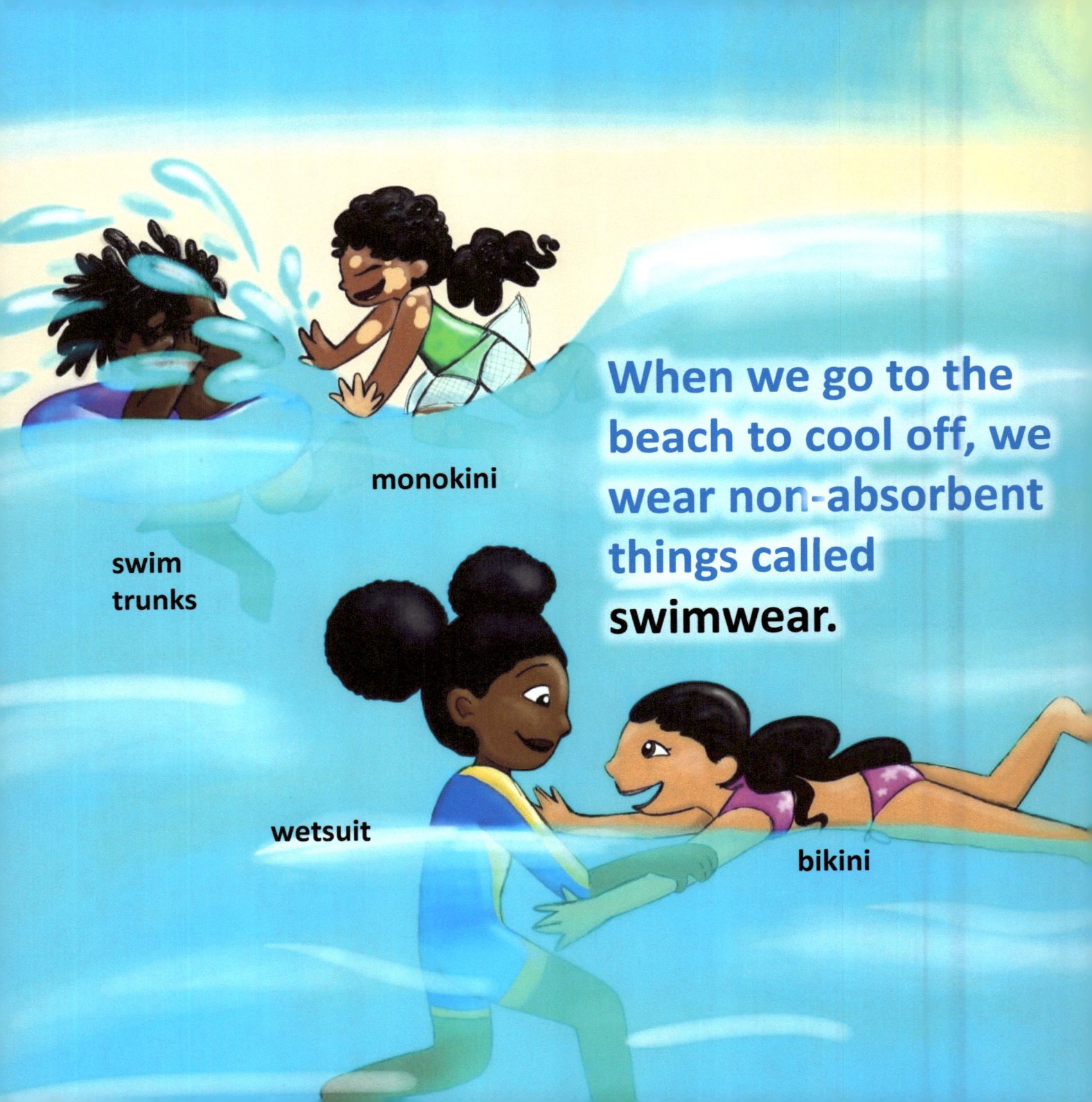

monokini

swim
trunks

wetsuit

bikini

When we go to the beach to cool off, we wear non-absorbent things called **swimwear.**

We wear things for safety. Kayla, Yasmin, and Sabeta wear **life jackets** when traveling by boat. Harriet and Taj use **goggles** in the lab. Sabeta wears **gloves** for beach clean up. Nelson wears a **reflective vest** to be seen in the dark.

life jacket

goggles

lab coat

mask

gloves

helmet

vest

We wear things under our clothes like **undershirts, camisoles,** and **underwear** to protect our skin and prevent body odor.

undershirt

underwear

We wear accessories such as ties, necklaces, bracelets, and rings for fashion. Watches tell the time. Boots protect our feet. Hats and sunglasses protect us from the sun. Belts and suspenders keep our pants on our waists.

bracelet

ring

necklace

suspenders

tie

watch

hat

glasses

boots

belt

Some children wear **uniforms** to identify the school to which they belong.

Uniforms help to create a sense of unity and prevent being bullied for dressing different.

When we finish our studies at school, we wear a **graduation gown** to the ceremony.

graduation gown

Some adults wear professional things to identify their occupation.

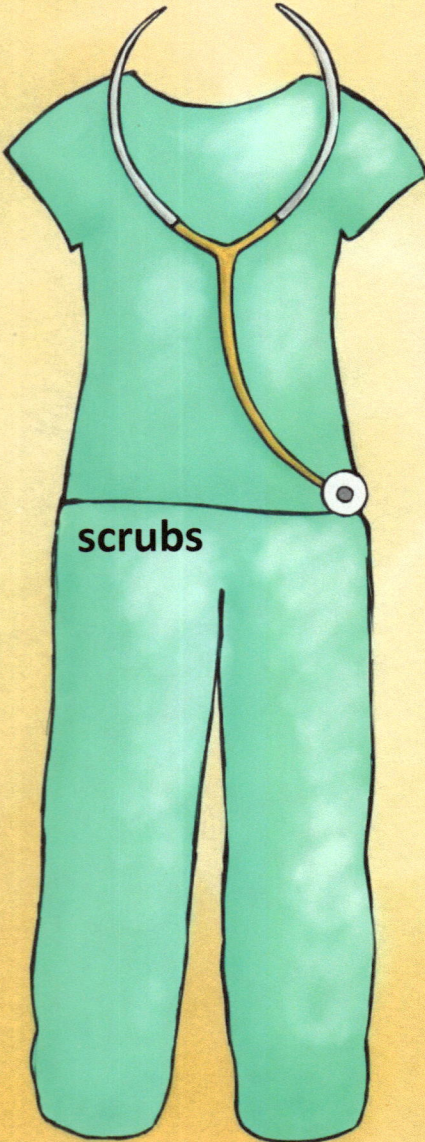

cap

stethoscope

scrubs

leotard

business suit

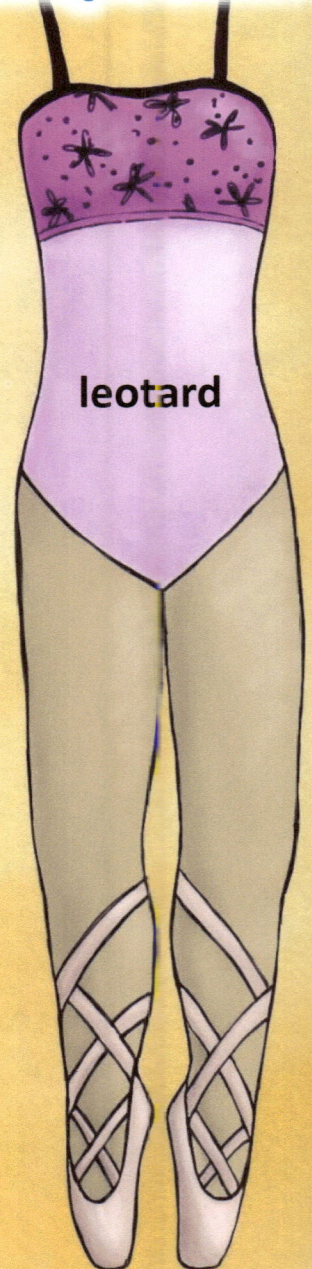

ballet shoes

We wear **pajamas** to bed. Some are thinner for the summer. Others are thicker to keep us warm in the winter.

Some people wear things to honor their faith and identify with their religion.

rastacap

fedora

bandeau

veil

burqa

habit

kāṣāya

kapoteh

We wear traditional things to show our cultural pride. Barak wears things that identify him as Jewish. Sabeta wears things that identify her as Native American.

kippah

tallit

suit

beaded regalia

trade skirt

moccasins

Engaged couples wear formal things on their wedding day. Brides wear **bridal gowns** or traditional dresses. Grooms wear suits or traditional men's wear.

We also wear special clothing to show national pride. Vera's parents are from China. They wear the traditional Chinese hanfu. Vera often wears a t-shirt and jeans.

pants

t-shirt

hanfu

jeans

Indira's family is from India. Her mom wears a **sari** or a **lengha choli**. Indira enjoys dressing like her mom. She says it makes her feel like a princess. Her dad wears a **bandhgala** on special occasions.

bandhgala

sari

Nelson's family is from the Yoruba people of Nigeria. They wear brightly colored clothing called dashiki. His mom wears a headscarf called a gele. His dad wears a hat called a kufi.

kufi

gele

buba

boubou

sokotos

Adam's heritage is Irish and Scottish. His mother wears the **leine** under an open sleeved **dress**. His father wears the **leine** under a **tweed jacket with pants or a skirt** called a **kilt**.

leine

dress

shorts

jacket

pants

Xavier's parents are from Japan. His parents wear **Japanese kimonos**. Xavier wears his **sports gear** every chance he gets!

sports gear

kimono

Yasmin's family is from Pakistan. Mom wears a traditional **dress** and dad wears

hijab

dress

salwar kameez

a salwar kameez, a long tunic worn over baggy pants. Yasmin wears a shirt and pants with a head covering called a hijab.

Abdulla's family is from the United Arab Emirates. His mother wears a long black **robe** called an **abaya** with a **hijab**. His dad wears a long white **tunic** called a **thawb** and a **headscarf** known as a **keffiyeh**. Abdulla dresses just like his dad.

keffiyeh

hijab

thawb

abaya

You do not have to be a model on the runway or travel the world to learn about the different things we wear. You can learn at your school, in your community, and from books like this!

Did you have fun exploring the different things we wear?

What is your favorite thing to wear?

What do you wear in the summer?

What do you wear for safety?

What do you wear that is not mentioned in this book?

Glossary

Boubou: French word for robe, kaftan, or a long loose fitting garment

Buba: A loose fitting blouse or shirt

Burqa: An outer garment that covers the entire body

Faux fur coat: A coat made from man-made material that resembles fur

Fedora: A wide rim hat

Kapoteh: A suit worn by Orthodox Jews

Kāṣāya: A robe worn by Chinese Buddhist Monks

Kippah: a skull cap worn by Jewish boys; also called **yarmulke**

Lengha choli: A long skirt with a top

Monokini: A one piece swimsuit

Nonabsorbent: Designed to not soak up or retain water

Parka coat: A coat with a warm lining

Pea coat: A short, double breasted jacket with large buttons

Puffer coat: A jacket padded with feather or fur

Sokotos: Drawstring pants

Tallit: a prayer shawl

Tradition: customs or beliefs passed from generation to generation

Biographies

Olivia Lauren, born in Farmington, Connecticut, is a 9 year old girl who enjoys writing stories and drawing. When she isn't writing stories, she is acting or modeling on the runway. Learn more on Instagram @olivialaurenj

Melissa-Sue John is a Jamaican born, psychology professor, mother of two girls, wife, author, and publisher of children's literature. Her goal is to create diverse, educational, and fun children's literature, coauthored with child authors and illustrated by youth illustrators. Follow @laurensimonepubs

Simonne-Anais Clarke is curious, optimistic, and creative teen. She is passionate about sharing stories with others through her art. She also enjoys writing stories, acting, and singing.

Zachary-Michael Clarke loves animated movies, writing stories, and creating graphic novels. He is excited to learn more about animation. He also enjoys learning how to cook gluten-free foods.

Read More Olivia Lauren Books

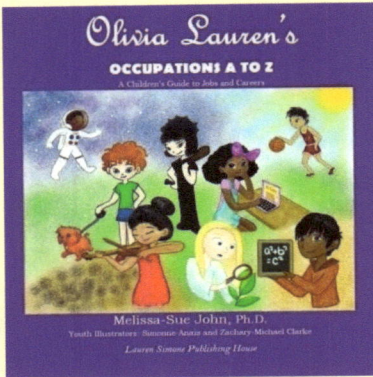

Occupations A to Z: A Guide to Jobs and Occupations
By Melissa-Sue John
Illustrated by Simonne-Anais and Zachary Michael Clarke

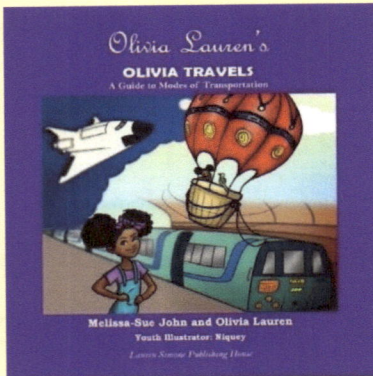

Olivia Travels: A Guide to Modes of Transportation
By Melissa-Sue John and Olivia Lauren
Illustrated by Niquey

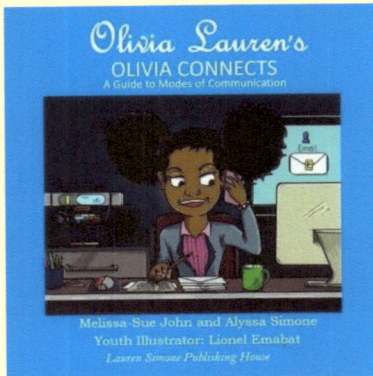

Olivia Connects: A Guide to Modes of Communication
By Melissa-Sue John and Alyssa Simone
Illustrated by Lionel Emabat

www.ingramcontent.com/pod-product-compliance
Lightning Source LLC
Chambersburg PA
CBHW040021050426

42452CB00002B/82